In Search of
DEMOCRACY

STEPHEN MCDOWELL & MARK BELILES

Providence Foundation

Charlottesville, Virginia

In Search of Democracy

Published by:
Providence Foundation
PO Box 6759
Charlottesville, VA 22906
804-978-4535
Website: www.providencefoundation.com

The Providence Foundation is a non-profit educational organization whose mission is to spread liberty, justice, and prosperity among the nations by educating individuals in a biblical worldview. The Foundation studies the relationship between religion and public life and offers numerous seminars, presentations, books, tapes, and other materials on the subject.

ISBN 1-887456-09-0

Printed in the United States of America

Contents

The Cry for Democracy

In recent years millions of Eastern Europeans, Russians, Chinese, and other peoples have demonstrated and cried out for freedom. They equate freedom and democracy and think democracy is necessary to correct the problems in their nation. But many people do not really know what democracy is or what makes it work. There are certain principles that can be derived from attempts at democracy in world history that we must learn or else suffer from the awful mistakes that others have already experienced in trying to establish a free government.

The cry for democracy is common to many countries in the world today. Millions of people from every race and culture recognize the need for reformation of their society. Over one-third of the world's population (2.1 billion people) live in poverty. Five hundred million live on the edge of starvation. One hundred and ten countries have been documented as violating basic human rights even to the point of torture. The number of people killed by their own totalitarian governments in the 20th century exceeds the number killed by war by almost four to one. The annual number of refugees in the world is about twenty-eight million. Added to these grim statistics are international terrorism, debt, crime, the threat of nuclear war, and escalating military conflicts.

In the face of such problems there is a movement all over the world toward *democracy*. On every continent there are multitudes saying that this is their desire. However, the term democracy has different meanings to different people, and therefore needs definition and explanation.

Many people associate the concepts of freedom and democracy as one and the same. But, in reality, freedom is what democracy exists to protect. Protection of individual rights and liberties is the goal, but democracy is the means. Certain rights are recognized by all people as inalienable — that is, they can never be denied to anyone without injustice. Such rights as freedom of religion, freedom of speech, freedom of assembly, freedom of the press, freedom of petition, and freedom of self-defense are of this nature. All inalienable rights can be summarized in three categories: the right to life, the right to liberty, and the right to property. All human beings recognize that to kill, steal or oppress another person is wrong, whether it is done by an individual or by governmental force.

The famous American President, Abraham Lincoln said that, "We all declare for liberty; but in using the same word we do not mean the same thing. . . . The shepherd drives the wolf from the sheep's throat, for which the sheep thanks the shepherd as his liberator, while the wolf denounces him for the same act. . . . Plainly, the sheep and the wolf are not agreed upon the definition of liberty." Lincoln said that some believe liberty means, "that each individual in the society may do as he sees fit with himself and the earnings from his labors." While others believe "that some persons may do as they see fit with other person's labors."

True liberty is not unbridled license. Government must provide a system of justice to address grievances while protecting the inalienable rights of individuals in the society. Therefore, the same authority structure that governs the people must also restrain the government itself.

Democracy literally means rule by the people. World history shows that when people rule their government, their rights are safer than when governed by one man or a few men. Centralized power in the hands of a few can be corrupted very easily. But it is also true that power in the hands of many people can also be corrupted.

Pure democracy as attempted by Greece in ancient history and France 200 years ago has proven to be not only impractical but also dangerous. Where people rule directly, they tend to favor the will of the majority at the expense of individual rights of minorities. Tyranny, therefore, can be found in pure democracy. It can become "mob rule" and endures only until threatened minorities finally join together against the majority using force to protect themselves. The result is chaos and anarchy, such as seen in the "reign of terror" in France after their revolution, and order is usually restored only by a totalitarian government, as occurred in France with Napoleon Bonaparte. This cycle also occurred in Greek and Roman attempts at democracy.

The father of the Constitution of the United States, James Madison, noted in *Federalist No. 10* that "democracies have ever been spectacles of turbulence and contention; have ever been found incompatible with personal security or the rights of property; and have in general been as short in their lives as they have been violent in their deaths."

Pure democracy, therefore, is to be avoided. How? By the concepts of representation and fixed higher law, which are associated with the term "republic." A free government may better be termed a *representative democratic republic* or *constitutional republic*. Henceforth, these elements should be kept in mind when we use the general term "democracy." The names *democratic republic* or *representative democracy* or *constitutional republic* more accurately express what free governments should be called.

We need to define the practical aspects of democracy even further if we want to avoid the mistakes of other democracy movements of history. In the next section we will examine seven basic governmental structures that are necessary to protect and secure individual rights and liberties. This is the essential framework of a Constitutional Republic.

The Framework of a Constitutional Republic

Decentralization of Government

Since power residing in the people is a basic premise of democratic government, the government should be kept as close to the people as possible. This can be accomplished by establishing a small national government and strong local and regional governments. Such a division of powers will be a safeguard against the tyranny of centralization since it will allow the people to most fully participate in government and to keep watch over the flow of power through the governing officials.

History has shown that centralization of governmental power destroys the liberty and the rights of man. The way to have good and safe government is to divide the power among the people and the localities, instead of entrusting it to one body.

Civil government in a country should be subdivided into many levels (local, regional, national). The power of each level should be clearly defined and sovereign in those defined areas. No level of government should be able to usurp the jurisdiction of another. A great majority of the power should rest on the local level.

The limited powers of the national government should be clearly defined in a constitution, and involve those things which affect the country as a whole, such as defense, foreign policy, regulation of interregional and foreign commerce, citizenship laws, coining money, and copyrights. All other powers should remain with the people, or with the local, and regional governments. The powers of local and regional government can be written in a regional constitution and include such things as traffic regulations, business regulations, public works, voting procedures, and law and order.

A constitution will enable the people to be able to see if the national government oversteps its authority. This usurpation of power can be resisted by the local and regional governments rallying together.

In a decentralized government a constitution, and not the national ruling party, is supreme. It should only be amended with the consent of the local and/or regional governments.

Constitutionalism

A government of liberty will be a government of laws, not of rulers or of the majority. In a pure democracy, a simple majority (just over 50%) of the people rule. The rights of the minority could be in jeopardy under such a government. Therefore, the best form of democracy will be a constitutional democracy. Here, the law is supreme, and protects the rights of all people.

Throughout most of history people have been governed by laws imposed by their rulers. In this they had no choice. In a democracy the people will form their own constitution and consent to it. Hence, they establish a government of people's law, not of ruler's law. Both the people and the rulers are subject to the law. This is essential for protecting the individual's rights to life, liberty, and property. Citizens must not only be protected from harmful acts of other citizens, but also from abuses by their own government. Since the law is supreme and not the rulers, the people will be protected from ruler's tyranny.

A constitution will define and limit the power of government. It acts as a chain to bind down rulers from misusing power. It is written so that it will not be forgotten.

Any government is free to the people under it, no matter what structure it has, where the laws rule, and the people are a party to those laws. Any government opposed to this will be one of tyranny.

A constitution formed by the people should not deny the rights of others. The laws will apply to all people equally, regardless of political position, religion, race, wealth, social status, or creed. Everyone is equal before the law in relation to protection of their life, liberty, and acquisition of property.

The source of the law of a nation will determine the degree of freedom and prosperity the people of that nation possess. The most democratic nations in history have had a law based in moral absolutes, which, in turn, have had their origin in religion. In reality, a people's religion is the source of their law.

Separation of Powers

A difficulty in forming any government where men are over men is that you must first enable the government to control the governed and then insure that the government controls itself. Men tend to abuse power, especially if they are given too much. It has been said that all power tends to corrupt; absolute power corrupts absolutely. Due to this tendency of abuse, power must be limited in our civil rulers.

We have seen that prescribing specific powers in a constitution is one way to accomplish this. Another way is to separate governmental powers into different branches with different personnel running each branch. Every government (whether a monarchy, oligarchy, democracy, etc.) exercises these three functions: legislative — lawmaking, executive — enforcing and carrying out laws, and judicial — interpreting laws.

Separation of powers is a division of functions and personnel between the legislative, executive, and judicial departments. It is setting up three separate branches with prescribed separate functions (in a constitution), where no person should serve in any two branches at the same time. This serves as an internal control of abuse of governmental power. Since men are not angels and tend to lack self-control, separation of powers will guard against tyranny.

The French political writer, Montesquieu, wrote in *The Spirit of Laws* (1748):

> When the legislative and executive powers are united in the same person, or in the same body of magistrates, there can be no liberty; because apprehensions may arise, lest the same monarch or senate should enact tyrannical laws, to execute them in a tyrannical manner. Again, there is no liberty, if the judiciary power be not separated from the legislative and executive. Were it joined with the legislative, the life and liberty of the subject would be exposed to arbitrary control; for the

judge would be then the legislator. Were it joined to the executive power, the judge might behave with violence and oppression.

Tyranny will result when legislative, executive, and judicial powers are all accumulated in the same hands, of one, a few, or many. This is also true of all rulers, whether hereditary, self-appointed, or even elected. Simply giving power to the people and allowing them to elect their leaders is not an assurance of securing liberty for all. One thousand despots would be as oppressive as one. We do not want to establish an elective despotism. Separating governmental powers into three branches is one of many controls on the government needed to keep the people's rights and liberties from being endangered.

The three branches should be independent of each other with no one branch having total control of another. As an example, the legislative branch should not be able to remove the executive or judiciary very easily; and the executive should not be able to dissolve the legislative or judiciary. While independent, these branches should not be completely separate, but should band together through a system of checks and balances. This will permit each branch to guard against one department encroaching into another, which would result in tyranny.

An example of checks and balances is the executive having the right to veto laws passed by the legislature, and the legislature being able to override the veto with a larger percentage vote by their members.

A well-defined system of checks and balances will help maintain the separation of powers in three branches. While a separation of powers will produce some conflict between the branches of government, this will assist in preserving the three branches of government and the system of checks and balances. To preserve them is as necessary as to institute them.

Trial by Jury

In a nation under law, any violation of the law requires a judge. Wrongdoers must be punished and required to make restitution to deter crime, yet, there must be an orderly process of justice where the guilty and innocent are distinguished. Judges should not only be knowledgeable of the law, but also honest, refuse bribes, and not show favoritism.

History is replete with examples of judges manipulated by government authorities to further their political agenda. An independent judiciary is essential to ensure that the written boundaries established by a constitution are maintained. The judicial system should be made up of individuals who will not be swayed by political pressures. Having unelected judges is one possible way of reducing those pressures.

The courts are not only the means of providing citizens due process of law, but they are also the ones who keep an eye on the legislative and executive branches of government and determine their faithfulness to constitutional standards.

Individual judges, even if unelected, may at times be manipulated by other government leaders to render unjust decisions against political opponents of the government. Therefore, in order to protect individual liberty, and guarantee a fair trial, there needs to be a judicial system that uses a jury drawn at random from society. These jury members should generally be on the same social level as the defendant. They also should be from the same city or geographical area as the defendant, yet should not know any facts about the case in advance that might color their perspective. The jury must be protected against government reprisals themselves in order to be independent. A jury of peers should be effective because it can judge of the defendant's character and the credibility of the witnesses. (Citizens must be knowledgeable and moral for trial by jury to work well. Individual characteristics are examined in the section on *The Essential Foundations of Democracy*.)

There is freedom in a society that guarantees that neither life, liberty, nor property can be taken from the possessor until a dozen or so of his countrymen shall pass their sentence upon oath against him. Government becomes arbitrary without such a system of justice. The legislature could pass oppressive laws or a judge could deliberately misinterpret the law.

The jury system was first found in British law over 1000 years ago. Governments, both fascist and communist, have forbidden trial by jury. The United States, in contrast, conducts about 120,000 jury trials each year.

Civilian Control of Police and Military Forces

Military and police power is a necessity in society to protect citizens from criminals and enemies, both foreign and domestic. A wise and prudent people will always have a watchful and jealous eye over this power. The American statesman, Thomas Jefferson, said that "the supremacy of the civil over the military authority" is an "essential principal" of democracy. His draft of the Declaration of Independence condemned the British King for rendering "the Military independent of and superior to the Civil" authorities, and also for keeping "standing Armies without the consent of our people. "

World history has proven repeatedly that armies that are supposedly the "people's", that is, there to protect the people's interests as a whole, are in reality being used by powerful government leaders to further their goals. Many nations experience military coups regularly and the generals of the armies run the nation rather than "presidents" and "constitutions."

In order to ensure civilian control of the military, a constitution should establish an elected head of state ("president") as the commander-in-chief of the armed forces in war time. However, rules for the military should be established by elected representatives of the people other than the head of state. These elected representatives should not be able to spend money for armies for more than the period of time until they face re-election. This keeps the support of the military power subject to the approval of the people, via their representatives.

As a means of decentralizing power and keeping local control, the officers of the armies should not be appointed by the head-of-state but by elected representatives from their own geographical area. The majority of a nation's army should simply be working citizens who have their own weapons and can be called together quickly. By doing this, no large permanent army can exist that can be taken control of by a political leader. This system allows any citizen to own his own weapon, which will give everyone the ability to defend himself, and will also give a geographic area of people the ability to defend themselves from armies that do become pawns of the government.

The police force should be locally and regionally controlled and completely separate from military power. The heads of the police forces should be elected and governed by local government. The rest of the police should be hired by the government as employees.

A Free Market Economy

The components of a free market economy are a basic necessity for any country that desires to secure individual liberty and economic productivity. In fact, a free market economy is the natural result of ideas of liberty. Components of a free market economy include private property rights, individual enterprise, and a free market.

Private property includes all things that belong to an individual that were acquired through his own labors or which had been freely given to him. This includes land, homes, personal possessions, inventions, wages, writings. Man does not only have a right to material property, but he also has a right to "internal property"— that is, he has a right to freedom in his religious beliefs, his opinions, his speech, and his writings.

Life and liberty are of great value to preserve, but without property rights they will soon be lost. If the people have property, they will have power to secure their rights to trial by jury, liberty of the press, freedom of worship, and others. Therefore, a primary object of civil government is the security of property (both internal and external) for its citizens.

The basic idea of *individual enterprise* is that citizens should be free to keep the rewards of their individual labor. When people are free to acquire and own property, produce what they want, choose their occupation, live and work where they wish, acquire whatever goods and services they desire, and have access to free markets they will prosper, and, consequently, cause their nation to prosper. Government should allow the people these freedoms.

In a *free market* people offer quality goods or services that are produced by their special talents and that they feel will be a benefit to the community. Each person is free to sell or not to sell at whatever price they want to offer, but they cannot force anyone to buy. Exchange of goods and services is voluntary and will occur as all involved believe they benefit from the exchange.

The prices of goods and services will be determined by "supply and demand." In a free market the supply of goods and services will balance out the demand for those goods and services, and these will be at a price the buyer and seller both agree upon. The greater the supply of any particular kind of good or service, the more the price will tend to go down. The greater the demand for any kind of good or service, the more the price will tend to go up. The government must refrain from interfering in the free market by setting prices and wages, but must protect the free market by punishing theft and fraud, and by enforcing contracts that were entered into freely.

A government must protect the people's property from unprincipled citizens, but must also constrain itself from taking the people's property or prohibiting individual enterprise and the free market. Following are a few ways the government can be constrained:

1. The constitution should guarantee private property rights, individual enterprise, and protect the free market.

   • Ways of doing this include setting a fixed standard of weights and measures (to keep the market fair), having copyright and patent laws (which encourage initiative and inventiveness), depriving no person of property without due process of law, and taking no private property for public use without just compensation.

2. Limited taxes, that are fair and equitable, should only be imposed by elected representatives who serve a short term in office before facing re-election. Taxing power of the government should be restricted for uses specifically enumerated in the constitution.

3. An honest money and honest banking system should be established, and deficit spending should only be allowed in emergencies. Fiat money, fractional reserve banking, and deficit spending are all inflationary and are a subtle way that government "steals" money from the citizenry.

Election of Representatives

Besides all the other safeguards against tyranny — decentralizing and separating government powers, establishing trial by jury, a civilian-controlled military, etc. — there is still one crucial part left in the framework of democracy. Although those governmental powers and offices are severely limited and checked, the men who are to fill those positions must be elected by the people and forced to face those same people frequently in order to be re-elected. This establishes accountability.

Frequent elections are essential, but also it is vital that the elections be free. This means that those who run for office can do so without restriction of being from one party. One party may possibly dominate elections but it must come through winning the battle in the free marketplace of ideas. The right of any citizen to form a party and offer candidates for election is essential.

The vote in a nation must not be compulsory if it is to be free. It must be voluntary, plus it must be available to all citizens equally, regardless of race, color, social status, religion or gender. The vote must also be by secret ballot so that no pressure nor fear of reprisal can influence the outcome.

Once the election determines the winner, there must be a commitment to the peaceful transition and relinquishing of power by the previous office-holders. It is essential also that all competing candidates and parties work to be unified for the common good of the nation.

It is important, however, that not all government offices be filled by popular choice. In order to prevent the politicalization of the judiciary, for example, it would be best that judges remain appointed by elected representatives.

Another safety necessary to prevent majority tyranny and ensure more healthy gradual change in a nation would be for different portions of the legislative and executive branches, on both the national and regional levels, to be up for elections on different years. This would prevent radical changes from taking place without time for the electorate to fully weigh the potential consequences.

The Sources of Democracy

Civil liberty has progressed on a slow and rocky path. From the time family groups and tribes first formed into nations with organized civil structures, the tendency has been to centralize power. People unwisely tend to put their trust in the state and collective political power rather than in themselves and in God, Who is the source of all things. The ancient empires of Assyria, Babylonia, Egypt, Greece, Rome and China are examples of this. It has taken thousands of years to convince men that utopian ideas of centralized government remaining just and incorrupt are unrealistic.

The governments of every ancient civilization, with the exception of the Hebrew Republic, "rested on the assumed natural inequality of men. The individual was regarded as of value only as he formed a part of the political fabric, and was able to contribute to its uses, as though it were the end of his being to aggrandize the State. This was the pagan idea of man. The wisest philosophers of antiquity could not rise above... the idea that man was made for the State" (Richard Frothingham, *The Rise of the Republic of the United States*). They were convinced that power should rest in the hands of one or a privileged few, who would then fashion the thought and control the action of the many.

Throughout history there has been a steady development of democratic ideas, which are in contrast to those above. We will highlight the main advancements.

The Hebrew Republic

The first genuine example of democratic government in world history is found in the Hebrew Republic established by Moses around 1300 B.C. This great emancipator provided a complete system of written civil law that was in great contrast to the ancient civilizations at that time. All other governments in the world centralized power in the hands of a king or emperor, but Moses set up a government with most powers decentralized.

He established a civil body which governed the nation and was composed of both elected and unelected officials. The ·Hebrew Republic was the first government in history to allow the people the freedom to elect their representatives. These representatives, furthermore, were limited in their decisions and actions by an absolute written moral and civil code known as the law of Moses which included the "Ten Commandments."

All of these representatives, elected or unelected, were not allowed to govern without an official agreement or covenant with the people to abide within the guidelines of the written code. This covenant ceremony, established by an oath before God, was the origination of the principle that governments "derive their just powers from the consent of the governed." Government based on agreement with the people was the origin of constitutionalism.

Three major principles were established here: decentralization, election of representatives, and constitutionalism. Once the Hebrew Republic was conquered by other empires there was not another complete example of these principles practiced by any nation in history until the establishment of the United States of America three thousand years later.

Greece and Rome

The second major attempt at democratic government in history was in the Greek city-state of the sixth century before Christ. The Athenian lawgiver, Solon, drew up a legal system that would allow the people to make their own laws. Plato and Aristotle emphasized that a just society was one where every man is moved by concern for the common good. These concepts were also embraced by Roman statesmen such as Cicero and Seneca in the second century before Christ. They proposed an impartial system of laws based on Natural Law which, Cicero said, comes from God and originated before "any written law existed or any state had been established."

While promoting some measure of civil liberty, the Greek and Roman theories were never as democratic as the Hebrew because of their belief in the inequality of men. The ideas of democracy and freedom were only extended to certain classes and all others were denied basic rights. Such tyranny eventually produced conflicts in society that led to chaos and disorder. Cicero was murdered and the government reverted to complete totalitarianism to restore order. Greek and Roman contributions to democratic ideas were more theoretical than actual, but were helpful to later generations who learned from their mistakes.

The fundamental flaws of their attempts at democracy were rooted in their belief that men were naturally unequal and that only one or a privileged few were competent to govern the rest.

Christianity

A few hundred years later, Jesus Christ began to reassert the basic Hebrew concepts of equality and liberty. Through his death and the commission He gave to His followers to teach these things to all nations, the march of democracy took a major leap forward.

Christianity emphasized that, in the eye of God, all men are equal. This asserted for the individual an independent value regardless of political contribution or social class or race. It occasioned the great inference, that man is superior to the state.

Jesus specifically taught that government rulers are to be public servants. Instead of people serving government, it ought rather be fashioned to provide justice and protection for them. Government should provide this service equally to all. This idea has effected many nations today, which is reflected in their use of the word *minister*, meaning *servant*, for top civil rulers.

The Christian view of man and government was a significant contribution toward democracy that made what Greece and Rome failed to achieve a possibility for future nations. The early Christian churches also established a model of self-government and unity with diversity that provided order without sacrificing freedom.

Britain

Although all of Europe was Christianized, it was the unique isolated situation of the British Isles that enabled some of the kingdoms and nations there to develop their democratic institutions without interference from surrounding nations. Patrick, a Christian missionary to Ireland in the fifth century, not only spread the Christian faith but also compiled civil laws from the Bible by which kings could rule, called *Liber Ex Lege Moisi* or *Book of the Law of Moses*. The Irish and, later, the Anglo-Saxon governments began to establish democratic institutions. Patrick's *Liber* influenced the greatest Anglo-Saxon king, Alfred the Great, to copy from the Hebrew model in his Code of Laws in the late ninth century. He set an example of a king who truly saw his role as one of serving the people.

The Anglo-Saxons originated the Common Law, trial by jury, and habeas corpus. In addition, they established an elected representative body called the "Witen". Though conquered by the Normans in 1066, the march toward democratic government was revived at Runnymeade when King John was forced to sign the Magna Charta. This document, drafted by the Christian clergyman Stephen Langton in 1215, affirmed in written form the basic rights such as representation, private property, and trial by jury.

The Protestant Reformation in Europe

Well over a century before Martin Luther, John Wycliffe was planting the seeds for the reformation of Europe. This Christian clergyman in 1382 translated the Bible into the common English language so that people would read it and establish, in his words, "a government of the people, by the people, and for the people." By the early sixteenth century similar translations had been completed in Germany, France, and other European countries. The Bible in the hands of the people not only produced religious reformation but also political reformation. The writings of Protestants such as John Calvin, Samuel Rutherford, and the Huguenots led finally to the English Bill of Rights in 1628 and the establishment of the first true democracy in modern history among the European exiles in America.

These exiles, having no other government to contend with in the New World, were the first free men to form their own government by consent through the signing in 1620 of what is known as the Mayflower Compact.

America

The Mayflower Compact was just one of about 100 different constitution-like documents drafted by the 13 colonial governments in America over the 150 year period preceding the American Revolution. The first constitution in history resulting in the establishment of a new commonwealth was written for Connecticut in 1638 by the Christian clergyman Thomas Hooker. The first "Bill of Rights" in America was written by another clergyman, Nathaniel Ward, for Massachusetts in 1641.

The Declaration of Independence, drafted by Thomas Jefferson and approved by the Continental Congress in 1776, was the most significant national document in modern times that articulated democratic ideas to their fullest extent. Thirteen years later these ideas were established institutionally in the United States Constitution. This document, the oldest continually operating constitution in the world today, established the framework of a Constitutional Republic with all seven of the elements mentioned in this study.

The Enlightenment in Europe

In Europe the Protestant Reformation gave rise to a movement of free-thinking men who continued to influence that continent toward democracy. The English Bill of Rights was written in 1689, which established the supremacy of England's representative body known as Parliament. A year later Englishman John Locke wrote his *Second Treatise on Civil Government*. Locke was influenced by various writings including John Calvin's *Institutes of the Christian Religion* (1536) and the French Protestant document *A Defense of Liberty Against Tyrants* (1579) by Philippe Du Plessis-Mornay. Locke's writings on resistance to tyrants was similar to the works of the Scottish reformer/clergyman Samuel Rutherford who wrote *The Law and the Prince* (1644). Other important European works included *The Rights of*

War and Peace (1625) by Hugo Grotius of Holland and *The Law of Nature and Nations* (1729) by Samuel de Puffendorf of Germany. In France *The Spirit of Laws*, written by Baron Von Montesquieu in 1748, articulated very effectively the principle of the separation of powers into three branches with checks and balances.

Others with a more secular approach, like Rousseau and Voltaire, were also influential, especially in France. The French Revolution, with its *Declaration of the Rights of Man*, occurred shortly after the American Revolution but had entirely different results. It followed the chaotic pattern similar to pure democratic efforts back in Greece and Rome. The "Reign of Terror", a result of mob rule, was brought to an end only by the restoration of totalitarianism under Napoleon Bonaparte.

Many other revolutions have occurred around the world since then and numerous constitutions have been written and rewritten with little real effect. Over one hundred and sixty constitutions exist in the world today and all but fourteen were written in the last forty years. The average life-span of a constitution today is fifteen years. It is often set aside when a military coup or popular revolt takes place. Many countries recognize the powerful idea of democracy and offer elections, but they are often not really free, for in effect the ruling party eliminates all choice in the contests.

How can we avoid the pitfalls that many peoples have already suffered through? What are the missing parts necessary for success that have eluded many countries who have experienced a revolution such as France had 200 years ago?

A French political philosopher, named Alexis De Tocqueville, offered some insightful answers about 150 years ago that coincide with statements by the Founders of the successful American experiment in democracy. They both pointed to some foundational principles essential to support the framework of a Constitutional Republic. Without these, they said, democracy will not work.

The Essential Foundations of Democracy

We have looked at structures that have been part of the best and most free governments in history. However, we must remember that good structures are not enough because the best government in ill hands can do nothing great or good.

The following principles must be part of the lives of the people of any nation desiring freedom and prosperity, for after all, it is men who cause governments to run. Governments depend upon men more than men depend upon governments. If men are good, the government will not be bad.

Self-Government

When people hear the word government they usually think of civil government for in most nations that is *the* government. In a general sense government means direction, regulation, control, restraint. There are many spheres of government each providing direction, regulation, control, and restraint in its jurisdiction. The spheres of government can be divided into internal and external government. Another name for internal government is self-government. All government begins internally in the heart of man, with his ability to govern his conscience, will, character, thoughts, ideas, motives, conviction, attitudes, and desires. How a man governs himself internally affects his external actions, speech, conduct, use of property, etc. Each external sphere of government is a reflection of the internal sphere. In other words, the internal is causative to the external. The type of government that exists in the homes, churches, schools, businesses, associations, or civil realms of a country is a reflection of the self-government, or lack of self-government, within the citizens.

The seventeenth century Dutch scholar, Hugo Grotius, who systematized the subject of the Law of Nations, summarized the principle of self-government in the following quote:

> He knows not how to rule a kingdom, that cannot manage a Province; nor can he wield a Province, that cannot order a City; nor he order a City, that knows not how to regulate a Village; nor he a Village, that cannot guide a Family; nor can that man Govern well a Family that knows not how to Govern himself; neither can any Govern himself unless his reason be Lord, Will and appetite her Vassals; nor can Reason rule unless herself be ruled by God, and (wholly) be obedient to Him.

Stated another way, you must rule yourself before you can rule others. There are many civil government leaders today who are attempting to govern their nation, yet are unable to effectively direct and control their own lives or their families.

Grotius' statement reveals how the flow of power should occur within a country, from the internal to the external. He speaks of decentralized governmental units wielding less power the further removed they are from the individual. The following chart summarizes his ideas:

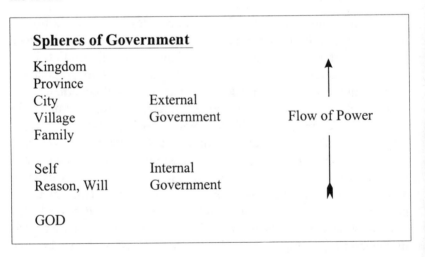

Spheres of Government

Kingdom		
Province		
City	External	
Village	Government	Flow of Power
Family		
Self	Internal	
Reason, Will	Government	
GOD		

Effective government begins by an individual learning to govern himself. The more internal self-government a person possesses, the less external government he needs. Consequently, the more rules and laws required to keep people acting rightly is a revelation of a diminishing amount of self-government. History teaches that man can control himself, but only to a limited degree. Since self-government cannot be imposed externally, and man is limited in personal self-discipline, there needs to be another source for internal control. Grotius reveals that man can only be truly self-governed if his reason, will, and appetite are ruled by God. The basis of self-control is obedience to the Creator and His standards of conduct.

As people in a nation become less self-governed, and give up power, the civil government (especially the national government) will grow and grow, making more and more laws (many outside its realm of jurisdiction) and spending more and more money. Lack of self-government leads to greater centralized external government.

Union

The people of a free nation will not only be self-governed but will also voluntarily work in union with each other for the common good of the entire nation.

The external union of a people results from an internal unity of ideas and principles residing in the hearts of the people. Compulsory union, that imposed by external force and fear, will never last. Union cannot be forced externally, but must arise from internal unity. An understanding of the principles and framework of a democracy must be inculcated in the hearts of all the people for a nation to remain together in union.

Covenant or compact among people on a local level is the basis of political union. For people to covenant together, they must share common beliefs, purposes, ideas, and faith. Joining together for civil purposes begins with covenanting together for independent purposes, such as in homes, churches, schools, clubs, and various organizations. (Historically, the concept of political union resulted from Christians covenanting together in a church fellowship.) Union is also seen in the commercial realm in partnerships and corporations. Independent and commercial unions not only benefit the people directly involved, but also the general populace. If there is not unity with union on the independent and commercial levels, there can be no political union.

Stronger internal bonds within a people will produce a stronger union. A people working together in union will greatly strengthen a country.

The principle of union at work in the various spheres of government will build up the nation as a whole, while self-government in the people will assure that the rights of individuals are maintained as well. The principles of self-government and union must be kept in balance. Too much emphasis on union will result in centralism, while too much emphasis on self-government leads to disintegration of the nation.

Individuality

The principle of individuality reveals that each person is created by God and is unique and distinct. Each has a well defined existence with unique talents and abilities which fits him for a special purpose. All men are alike in many ways (there is a unity among mankind), yet no two men are alike (there is also diversity). Man has physical characteristics that make him unique, such as his fingerprints, profile, voice prints, scent, and nerve pattern on the inside of the eye. He also has unique internal characteristics, including thoughts, opinions, emotions, and attitudes.

Man is a reflection of his Creator, who is a unity (God is One), yet He is also diverse (God is a triune Being). God does not create carbon-copy molds of anything, whether humans, animals, trees, minerals, mountains, rivers, planets or stars. Everything He creates is unique and distinct, yet there is a unity among all things for God created them all.

Every person has his own outward and inward identity or individuality. Every person is responsible and accountable for their own choices and actions. For governments to be free, the people must assume this responsibility.

Man, being created by God with a unique existence, has an independent value. His value is not dependent upon his ability to contribute to the state. Man is of highest value and the state exists to serve man, rather than man serve the state. Man, therefore, is superior to the state. In a government that views the state as paramount, individuals' lives, liberty, and property will be in danger if they do not cooperate with or contribute to the state.

The principle of individuality further reveals that all men are equal. However, men are not equal in their talents and abilities, but they are equal in their right to life, liberty and the pursuit of acquiring property. Governments embodying false ideas of equality say men have an equal right to material possessions and thus try to distribute the wealth accordingly. All men have equal rights before the law. Governments exist in order to secure those rights.

A free government will keep a balance of unity with diversity. Too much emphasis on diversity leads to anarchy or freedom run wild. In such a state man will be self-centered, and lawlessness, license, and nihilism will be predominant. The resulting forms of government will run from anarchy to pure democracy.

Tyranny will result from an over-emphasis on unity. The rulers (or ruler) will center in on themselves and do as they please for their benefit or what they consider to be of benefit to the whole. The result is centralization of power and slavery and bondage to large groups of people. The forms of government that result from this mentality range from bureaucracy or collectivism (socialism, communism) to dictatorship. Here, the central government determines the rights and liberties of the people.

A balance of unity and diversity will produce liberty with order in a society and government by the consent of the governed. The resulting form of government will be a decentralized, democratic constitutional republic.

Property

A free market economy is one of the pillars of the framework of a democracy. The components of a free market economy — private property rights, individual enterprise, and a free market — flow from the principle of property in the lives of the people. A person's property is whatever he has exclusive right to possess and control. Property is first internal. A person's conscience is his most precious aspect of property because it tells him what is right and wrong in his actions. Each person in a free government must be a good steward of his conscience and keep it clear. By doing so, he will know what is right and wrong from within and, therefore, he will be able to live his life in a right manner.

How one takes care of his internal property will determine how he takes care of his external property. The following chart reveals various aspects of internal and external property:

Internal Property	**External Property**
Thoughts	Land/Estate
Opinions	Money
Talents	Freedom of Speech
Conscience	Bodily Health
Ideas	Possessions
Mind	Freedom of Assembly
Affections	

Governments exist to protect property of every sort, most importantly, liberty of conscience. Tyrannical governments will usually invade rights of conscience before invading external property rights. The power that can invade liberty of conscience, can also usurp civil liberty. Internal property rights must, therefore, be guarded at all costs, for as they are diminished, every inalienable right of man is jeopardized.

The famous British political scientist, John Locke, wrote in his treatise *Of Civil Government*:

> For Men being the Workmanship of one Omnipotent, and infinitely wise Maker. All the Servants of one Sovereign Master, sent into the World by His Order, and about His Business, they are His Property, whose Workmanship they are, made to last during His, not one anothers Pleasure.

Locke goes on to state that while we are God's property, God has given us the responsibility to be good stewards over our persons. He wrote that "every man has a Property in his own Person." It follows we have a God-given right to everything necessary to preserve our persons—to internal and external property.

Before any property can be taken from us, we must give our consent. If our property can be taken without our consent, then we really have no property. This is why any taxes imposed by a government on its citizens must be done by elected representatives. We give our consent to taxes or laws affecting our property rights through our representatives. If they do not represent our views, we should work to replace them in a lawful manner.

A people standing on the principle of property will take action to prohibit government or other citizens from taking anyone's personal property without their consent, or from violating anyone's conscience and rights. Lack of this principle in the lives of citizens will lead to unjust taxation, a government controlled economy, and usurpation of both internal and external property rights.

Education

An ignorant people will quickly become a people enslaved. Only a well-instructed citizenry can be permanently free. To preserve liberty in a nation, the general populace must understand the principles upon which a free government is based, for as they do, they will be able to prevent the leaders from eroding their constitutional rights.

Education is a sowing and reaping process. It is like a seed. The ideas that are sown in a people will grow over the years and produce fruit, manifesting in every aspect of life — personal, social, political, economic. That is why the philosophy of the schools in one generation will be the philosophy of government in the next.

What the educational institutions of a country teach lays the foundation for liberty or bondage, depending upon the ideas imparted. Education is the means for propagating a governmental philosophy. In recent years, where Marxists have taken over certain countries, one of the first things they have done is to assume control of the educational system and through that teach their ideologies and propagate their ideas.

Each form of government has its own philosophy of education. Public educational institutions will always teach the philosophy of the state. This is one reason why most education should be kept in the private sector. Any government or public schools should be decentralized and controlled on the local level. If the educational philosophy of a nation is changed, the governmental philosophy will change in the future.

For a free government to be sustained, the people must have an understanding of the working and structure of democracy. The people can then keep an enlightened eye on their civil leaders. However, education involves more than just acquiring knowledge or learning facts. Of greater importance is education in morals and principles. We have seen that the citizens of a nation that desires to be free and prosperous must be people of principle. Education in religion and morality is of first importance. Such education should not merely impart knowledge of morality, but actually implant morals and virtue within the people.

True education is the means for propagating free government to future generations. Without it, tyranny will reign.

Morality

No nation can long endure without virtue or morality in the people. A loss of principles and manners is the greatest threat to a free people and will cause its downfall more surely than any foreign enemy. While a people are virtuous they can not be subdued, but when they lose their virtue they will be ready to surrender their liberties to the first external or internal invader. The greatest security from enslavement in a country is virtue or morality among the people.

Everyone's fundamental rights are threatened by a lack of morality in the people. People of character will desire to observe the law and will not willfully take the life, liberty or property of others. Consequently, people will not live in fear of other citizens. In addition, less government will be required in a virtuous nation. Since fewer people will violate the law, a large police force and judicial system will not be needed. Law making bodies will also have less to do because prohibitive laws will be at a minimum, as citizens will constrain themselves.

In a virtuous nation the rulers will be moral. This produces more freedom because the rulers will not usurp individual rights through bad legislation and they will not steal from people through fiat money, excessive or graduated taxes, or other means. Consequently, people will not live in fear of civil government.

What is virtue or character? Virtue has been defined as a conformity to a standard of right, and also a voluntary obedience to truth. Character is a convictional belief that results in consistent behavior.

History has shown that such virtue and character in the people is the basis of happiness in a society and is absolutely necessary for a state to long remain free. As human nature is corrupted, the foundations of democracy are easily destroyed.

Following are some characteristics of virtuous citizens:
- They will have a concern for the common good above their own self-interest.
- They will vigorously participate in local, regional, and national government, and will seek to correct wrong conduct in public officials.
- If necessary, they will risk their life, fortune, and honor for their country.
- They will perform their duties and seek to have right conduct in public and private.

A free market economy is dependent upon the people being virtuous because such a people:
- Will not steal from their employees or others. Such theft increases the cost of goods and services for everyone.
- Will have a strong work ethic and be productive. This hard labor will cause the economy to grow.
- Will respect contracts.
- Will save and invest to acquire a greater return later.
- Will have a concern for their posterity and will seek to pass on a greater estate than they received.
- Will not waste public resources and will be good stewards of the environment.

A lack of character in the people can, therefore, produce a stagnant or declining economy, corrupt laws, a lack of smooth transition from one political leader or party to another after elections, a corrupt military who may take control of the government, and increased power in civil government, which results from its attempt to solve the many problems that arise from the lack of character in the people.

A virtuous people will be vigilant to work to establish a free nation and then also to maintain it. Eternal vigilance is the price to maintain liberty. People of character will be eternally vigilant to secure their rights and demand that their government's power remain limited.

Faith

The framework and foundational principles of democracy flow directly or indirectly out of the faith or religion of the people. Each one of the principles that must be a part of people's lives for democracy to be established and maintained require the indispensable support of the Creator.

With the principle of individuality, we saw that the uniqueness and value of man comes from his being created by God. Man becomes self-governing as he is subject to God and His truth. Morality cannot exist separate from religion. Man's most precious possession, his conscience, responds to right or wrong put in his heart by his Creator. The strongest force to bring union between a people is a common faith. Education that will propagate liberty must sow seeds of truth. All truth originates with God.

For the fundamental rights of man to be secure from government, the people must recognize that these rights are endowed by their Creator, and not granted by government. If people think that government, or man, is the source of rights then government can take away the rights of the people. But if God gives rights to men, then they are inalienable.

A fundamental question in securing liberty for all men is: "Who is the source of law in a society?" In reality, the source of law in a society is the god of that society. If man is the final source of the law, then the law will constantly change as man's ideas and understanding changes. God is the source of true law and His law is absolute. William

Blackstone, the great English legal scholar, said that no human laws are of any validity, if contrary to the higher law of God.

In studying the development of democracy, it is readily apparent that the Christian faith has provided laws that have produced the greatest amount of freedom and prosperity in history.

Christianity has produced the power or principles in the people for democracy, as well as the form or framework of democracy. Certain aspects of this law of liberty are revealed to all men, in what Blackstone called the Laws of Nature. However, the primary way that God has revealed His law to man is through the Bible, the written word of God. To the degree that nations have applied the principles of the Bible, is the degree to which those nations have prospered and been free.

The author of the first exhaustive dictionary, Noah Webster, stated:

> Almost all the civil liberty now enjoyed in the world owes its origin to the principles of the Christian religion. . . . The religion which has introduced civil liberty, is the religion of Christ and his apostles, which enjoins humility, piety, and benevolence; which acknowledges in every person a brother, or a sister, and a citizen with equal rights. This is genuine Christianity, and to this we owe our free constitutions of government.

Power and Form of Democracy

External forms always result from an internal power. This is true for civil governments, churches, homes, businesses, or associations. The power, which is internal, precedes the form, which is external.

Both a power and a form are needed for anything to function properly. The internal power is the life or energizing force and is essential for any form to work as it should; yet, a form is absolutely necessary to channel the power properly. We not only need power and form, but we also need a balance between the two. Too much form causes all involved to dry up, while too much power causes them to "blow up." Communism, for example, produces a form of civil government that relies almost totally on external pressure to keep everyone "in line." The internal creativity, life and motivation of each individual is suppressed and often dried up by these external constraints. An overemphasis on power leads to anarchy and eventually bondage. Historically, this can be seen after many national revolutions, the French being an excellent example.

We examined the form of a free government under the section on "The Framework of a Constitutional Republic." The principles examined in this section reveal the power of a free government. (Diagram 1 represents the Power and Form of a Free Government.) The form of democracy can only come forth and be maintained by a people that have the proper power or spirit within them. Without this foundation, a free government can never be established or maintained. It is not enough for a nation to copy some external form of government to secure liberty. That external form must flow out of the principles of liberty within the heart of the people. The pathway to liberty within a nation is from the internal to the external.

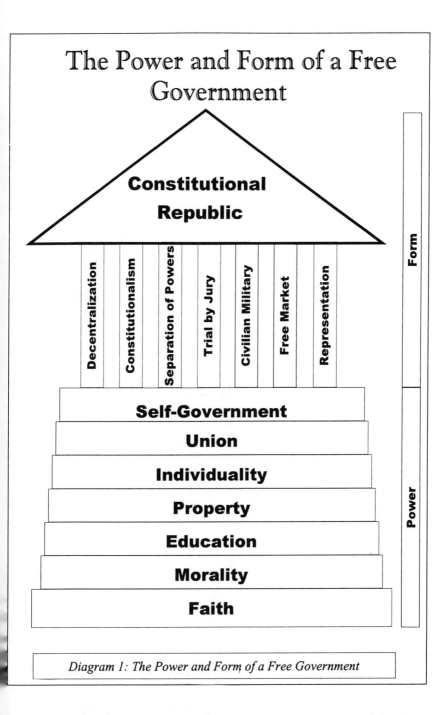

Diagram 1: The Power and Form of a Free Government